Is It Cloth, Clay, or Paper?

Andy Miller

ROSEN
COMMON CORE
READERS

Rosen Classroom™

New York

Published in 2013 by The Rosen Publishing Group, Inc.
29 East 21st Street, New York, NY 10010

Book Design: Michael Harmon

Photo Credits: Cover (jug) Hinatau Aliaksei/Shutterstock.com; cover (flowers) Sopotnicki/Shutterstock.com; cover (cloth) Yellowj/Shutterstock.com; p. 5 M. Dykstra/Shutterstock.com; p. 7 Karkas/Shutterstock.com; p. 9 Aleksandr Bryliaev/Shutterstock.com; p. 11 Gemenacom/Shutterstock.com; p. 13 Serg64/Shutterstock.com; p. 15 Albert Campbell/Shutterstock.com.

ISBN: 978-1-4488-8707-1
6-pack ISBN: 978-1-4488-8708-8

Manufactured in the United States of America

CPSIA Compliance Information: Batch #WS12RC: For further information contact Rosen Publishing, New York, New York at 1-800-237-9932.

Word Count: 66

Contents

What is this card made of?
It is made of paper.

Happy
mother's
day!!

What is this dress made of?
It is made of cloth.

What is this pot made of?
It is made of clay.

What is this shirt made of?
It is made of cloth.

What is this plate made of?
It is made of clay.

What is this flower made of?
It is made of paper.

Words to Know

card

dress

plate

shirt

Index